Feast

and

Famine

GW00503961

To Val,
with very best wishes
from

Feast and Famine

by

James Burch

Phygtyles Press
5, Bridle Lane
Downham Market
Norfolk PE38 9QZ

First published in 2005
PHYGTYLES PRESS
5, Bridle Lane,
Downham Market,
Norfolk, PE38 9QZ

e-mail: phygtylesress@eidosnet.co.uk
www.phygtylespress.co.uk

Printed by Poetry Monthly Press
39, Cavendish Road,
Long Eaton,
Nottingham, NG10 4HY

ISBN: 0-9545053-2-8
Copyright © James Burch 2005

CONTENTS

v

PART THREE
OTHER RECENT POEMS

Introduction

In my first published volume, *After October,* the poems all circled around a single theme, my wife Thea. The poems in the first half of that book looked at aspects of our life together, whilst those in the second half dealt with her death and my reactions to it. The present collection includes more such poems. These are in the second of the three sections, at the middle, or the heart of the book, where they belong. I have no doubt that it is a theme that I will return to again as long as I continue to write poems. Some people, I know, read *After October* as a continuous narrative. For them, these poems in the middle section of the present book will add to that story.

However, *Feast and Famine* has two other sections. The last of these contains poems written since Thea's death, but on various other topics. It might well be that in these poems too there are glimpses or echoes of Thea to be found, but that was not my deliberate, conscious intent in writing them. At the beginning of the book is a selection from poems written at, or about, various much earlier times. Some, but not all, of these are autobiographical.

The poems about Thea are as true and honest as I could make them. Many of the rest are true also, but others are part true, part exaggeration, part wishful thinking or pure invention.

ACKNOWLEDGEMENTS

From the times when the earliest of these poems were written until now is a considerable span of years. Some of the people for whose interest I have been grateful have appeared or, sadly, disappeared at various points throughout that period: others have been there throughout. Amongst individuals that come first to mind are Carolyn, Nick, Sarah, Pearl and Ned Irish, Anne Payne, Bill Wall, Jo Mullin and Diana Warwick. Groups that have, in their own distinctive ways, provided various blends of interest, encouragement, criticism, support, comment, advice, appreciation and insult include the: Downham Pub Poets, Fakenham Shed Poets, King's Lynn Writers' Circle, King's Lynn Centre Poets and Cambridge Writers' Poetry Group. Venues offering opportunities to read poems to a wider audience have been afforded by: the King's Lynn Festival, Wells-Next-The-Sea Poetry Festival, West Acre Theatre, Norwich Cafe Poets, Norfolk Radio and the Ostrich at Castle Acre. Some of the poems have appeared in the magazines: Poetry Monthly, The Penniless Press and Breathe. A couple were included in the King's Lynn Writers' Anthology, and different ones in each of two other anthologies, Twenty Poets at the Maltings and Close to the Edge. I would also like to take this opportunity to thank all of those who wrote to me about my first volume, *After October*. I have put a pretty full summary of your comments on my web-site www.phygtylespress.co.uk

To

Thea

Carolyn, Nick, Sarah and Pearl

Some Early Poems

Juvenilia

I read my old, young poems,
Full of claimed excesses,
Hormones at the door.
I wish I'd written more.

Past clamour now,
Not touched by wisdom's choice,
A few more years of shouting
Might have improved my voice.

Approach Road
The Birth of a Salesman

I saw her standing
From a very long way off,
Twenty-five or thirty years perhaps,
A distant dot shaping a landscape,
Small breasts, pushed by a rucksack,
Offering a mandate.

A lifetime of motor-miles
Logged and behind me,
Empty of savour,
Hardly to thought available.

Now, on my journey,
I saw words emblazoned
And, in a happy moment, wrote them
With felt tip across her T-shirt,
'The basis of a better life is sexual excess
- In moderation.'

We left the highway then at junction ten,
Rejoined at eleven, but straightway left again.

Parted at last with felt tip dry ,
My message smudged, our shirts and smiles awry.

Resumed a motorway suffused with sun and big with sky,
Minutely featured now, full of our history.

Brief Uncounter

You say, 'Goodbye,'
Whilst I rehearse, 'Hallo.'
Your eyes lose warmth,
Take thought,
Look further than they did.
You turn to where
A me-less future's hid.

Whilst I stand
Numbed
By what we both so swiftly know,
Your feet pass quietly,
Crisp, crisp,
Through the snow.

Gentleman's Excuse Me

The second
Or was it the third time I saw you,
Standing at my door,
I thought you were pregnant,
Though assuredly not by me.

That loose black coat,
Wan face,
And awkward stance,
Leaving your body, somehow,
Outside the room.

So it seemed a bad time
For me to make my move,
Claim my dance.
But I was wrong.
Pregnant you weren't.
Maybe the time was good.
Some sort of message received,
But message misunderstood.

Many times I thus botched my plans,
Stepping forward, half-rehearsed,
Faltering in, fantasy first,
Then signs discerned of orbital decay,
And watched your tumbling fall
Into some milkman's way.

Moving sadly in reverse,
Became a familiar exercise,
Hesitation raised to art,
A graceful touch,
But not the hero's part.

Now I hear
That you are out in the world,
Available again, perhaps,
And all my dreams, to catch your dreams,
Are stratagems, and traps
To bring you under arms,
And with soft skirmishes and sharp alarums,
Manoeuvre your retreat.
Anything less would be my twelfth defeat
And deep heart's ache.
For you, a friendly face,
Some talk, a drink, a lunch, a laugh,
And one more twirl, for old times' sake.

Just So Blonde

We crunch through brittle stalks;
Dark, dead, last year's stems of this year's food.
Shrinking their spiky touch,
You mime the graceful twists of winter wood.

You hide behind a non-concealing bush
And fail to foil my clutch, with a token push.
I catch and taste your laughing breath.
I hold you loose.
You beat me gently with your breasts.

The sun, escaping clouds beyond our trees,
Throws startling yellow on more distant ground
And, while by this year's dark-brown, ripe, dear girl held fast,
Come thoughts within the shallow reach of tears,
Too quick to dodge, unsubtle, un-profound;
The girl before the girl before this last,
Was just so distant, just so blonde.

She Will Not Break Your Heart

She will not break your heart,
Although your heart feels pain,
Although her words are cruel,
And bring your spirits low,
And madness comes again,
She does not mean to hurt,
And she would tell you so.

With everything she does,
Her thoughts are for your good,
Although your heart feels pain,
Although her words are cruel,
And bring your spirits low,
And madness comes again,
Her motive is to please,
As surely she will tell.

The blame cannot be hers,
To think so is unkind,
Although your heart feels pain,
Although her words are cruel,
And bring your spirits low,
And madness comes again,
To make you like a fool,
That was not her design.

Although she may depart,
And let you see her go,
She would not break your heart,
And she will tell you so.

Strings

He left in summer
To work alone,
Avoiding her sorrow
And pleas to return,
To follow a thought
And polish a tune.

She took another man.
It had not been her way.
Solitude surrendered.
Dark destroyed the day.
Winter stalked the woods
And took his cause away.

Through The Dark, Glassily

I did very little
To deserve my last, sharp memory of you.

Joined a midnight marauding party to the pool.
Discovered nude bathing was the order of the night.
Stripped off in darkness. Plunged morosely in.
Noticed a cool caressing slipstream round my crotch.
Thanked God sincerely for the absence of piranhas.
Witnessed a brief de-briefing of a don,
His briefs, and brief authority, soon gone.

Then, treading water at the deeper end, looked up
To see your silhouette upon the sky,
Legs slender together, bottom pouting out,
Arms apart, hands gripped upon the rails,
Breasts jutting gently, head hung back
And spine so softly arched, with hair cascading.

Remembrance stirred, of a thousand escalations,
Each past advertisement, its public, dim presentiment inflated,
Released emotions, secretly post-dated.
Chocolates, deodorants, away-day summer sights,
Cheap trips, exotic package tours, sports cars and tights,
Knitwear, footwear, fruits and tonic wine,
Swimsuits, stockings, curlers and bras,
Baited each with concubine,
All merged and lodged in store and now found ripe
To service my senses with their archetype.

A simple shape against the lightening sky,
Breaking the eyes' familiarity,
To start the chlorine stinging at my thigh.

Crossing The Sahara By Night

I knew it was down there
But
By night
Lacking a moon
Could only
In wonder
Dumber than usual
Dredging at memories
Write
And erase
And re-write
Phrases like,
'Ah,' and 'Oh,' and 'Lo,' and
Worst of all
'Invisibly inscrutable.'
Then cross them through
Then
Sourly
Write them down again.

Kano came soon
With bumps
A cool breeze
Jostling its warmth and damp.

Harmattan

Nose-picking time
They call it in school
When the red wind
Cool from the North
Fine with dust
Blows to a fog
Driving the drivers
Stirring stewards
Crazing them careless
Restless with static
Sparking at contact...

It gets to the colleges later,
Before their exams.

Bargains

With all my arts
Three times I break his last, best price.
The Niras plummet
But,
With eagle-swiftness,
Clench,
Leaving me fleeced,
The dangling victim.

A week later I try again.
'Forty,' he says, 'Good price.'
'Five,' I say, 'That's good for me.'
'I tell you,' he says, smacking his hands,
'Thirty five and finish.'
I stick at seven.
'But I pay twenty,' he protests,
'Last week, in Maiduguri.'
'Then you have saved me seven Nira
I really can't afford,' I say,
And walk, short-leashed, implacably, away.

But he folds his pack,
And Africa mocks.
The masks and trinkets
Smile at my yearning back.

Next day I bought them,
Meeting his price.
Now I have flown with them home.
Already I know they are bargains.
Feel fat
And rich
And mean.

The Down Rover

What a desperate dog this is.
Rib-snapper, gut worrier, howler in caverns,
Gruncher, growler.
I dip my eyes
And can see him,
Just,
A fierce, dark, snuffling, tearing, intestinal prowler.

Woolwich Ferry

Timbers heave and splash at the boat's approach.
Across the river, buildings of Silvertown await.
We could surprise them still by taking the tunnel,
But queue instead, to make a proper crossing.

Widely the ferries tick and dock their way across.
Ropes curl and stretch, and gangplanks clatter, fragile, into place.
The engines welcome us, warm at their windows, flaunting their parts.
Brasses smell and gleam. Ladders drop blackly into further depths.

The great cranks rear and plunge.

The decks are thick with people.

Out from the further bank
Another ship sets out,
A sister ship,
Complete with other travellers,
Other parts,
All interchangeable with us,
Carving its complementary route through different waters.

That boat could sink,
We to the rescue chase,
Churning our paddles, heavy in slow pursuit,
The authentic hero's crown brushing us by
But, still safe and dry, and counting our good luck,
Storing up sights and talk, competing in concern
With life-belt, raft and rope and frantic pointing,
And with charity to burn.

Or we could be there,
Down in the water,
Or clinging to a tilted deck,
Gazing with sullen envy through the spray
At all our snug, safe sisters.

Which step was it put me here,
To wonder wastefully with other lives?
And, as this broken engine steams and dies,
Scheduled these dreary, damp alternatives,
And tired conceits,
And tide-worn thoughts,
And trite surmise?

Burn Again Whittington

We had been discussing friendship,
How few the times the drifting sparks took fire.

We spoke of girls,
In Kensington, St Albans, Potters Bar.
But more
Of the lonely, night-time space
Between their doors.

We spoke of fatherhood,
Son-hood,
Roots
And drift,
Of bonds,
Carelessly broken,
Lifelines
Frayed by neglect,
Dangling useless,
In a time of wreck.

We paused by empty trains,
Some wretched and racked, bereft,
Others running wild,
Rearing away and up,
Their heads held curiously high,
Lamp-eyed,
Looming.

From Finsbury Park
We went our separate ways,
One to the splendours of his dreadful dark,
One to the routine terrors of his days.

Destry Rides Again

My nights were never safe.
You revelled in conspicuous disguise,
And posed and poster-hung my bed-sit walls
With poised, closed, knowing, tired lips
And bleak, up-glancing eyes.

Studied in dreams,
You sent your messages in easy codes;
A life presented as a picture book;
A body pacing the room in see-through robes;
Deeper enigmas sleeping in your look.

By now these illustrations should seem quaint,
But are not so. I am the boy again.
You worldly-wise; me still the fearful fool
Willing you to work out your designs,
And start your wickednesses sweet and cruel.

Crooked leg, black stocking, garter, flaunted thigh,
Twirl-away skirt to show the knee held high,
Your image still parades its gaudy shows.
Stalking you still, I proffer my fading gift;
Accepted, fondled, kissed,
My lovely, dew-dropped, fragrant, splendid, long stem
Rose.

Bed-Sit Safaris

In the centre,
A tall, deep space.
On each side of the space,
A wall.
And at each wall,
A figure,
Each figure
Busy.

One climbs,
With hook-like hands
And vigorous knees,
Towards the stars.
But, as the muscles stretch and stretch,
His skin sticks closer, closer,
Scrabbling the damp grit-friction.
Fear seeps in.

Another figure
Struts at a window,
Looking thoughtful
Into the corners of the room,
Pausing in profile,
Foot frowning,
Hair grasping,
Smiling at sudden thought,
Listening, and,
From the tiniest corner of his eye,
Peeping.

A third grows plants,
Spreads crumbs for birds,
Carefully browns his skin,
Hangs garlic and wind-chimes.

A fourth
Groans in desperate courtship
Of an undetermined shape
Glimpsed nightly through net curtains.

The central cavern,
Higher than ceilings,
Deeper than ground,
Echoes with heartbeats,
Carries the sound of winds
And the distant force of the sun,
Drops lower than sight,
Sucks at our bones,
Shows hurrying clouds,
And the pale pull, pull of the moon.

Mist At Six

Through morning's dark
Came pheasant's croak.

On that
    out there
        un-scene,

Ears trace day's break.

Winter Morning

Moon in the morning sky.
Not the remembered pale, grey tissue.

I arise at six
To suck hot tea

Then,
At the darkened window,
See this marbled, great, white blob,

Bold as night-time,

Doomed,

Brave in the face of dawn,

Sheeting the lawn,
Spitting out wormcasts.

Spatial Prejudice

Chastening really,
After all the rude things
I've said about our local flatlands,
Not fellscape or lakelands,
But grainlands,
Prairie,
With nary a tree
Or hill
That,
Driving again
Out of the lane,
Past that ever-snatching bramble,
Turning towards Barley,
A daily manoeuvre for fifteen years,
There, on the horizon,
High on the horizon,
I see a wooded ridge,
A well-treed headland,
Sticking up,
Conspicuous indeed.

It's the same every day now.
I find on the map
It's a tail end of Chiltern.
I still can't believe it.

And,
How does one start again
With a once familiar
Now uppity landscape?

Are apologies demanded?
Somehow I'd rather Martians had landed.

Scene From The Train

They looked at first
Like turds,
Dropped so neatly
Down the lines of stubble,
Then like eyebrows,
Each with a corner raised
And pointing.

But they were pheasants,
Soon,
When flushed,
To rise like startled laughter,
Fall like frowns.

Of Tits And Trees

Mornings like these
I think my brains
Must be in my wrists.

I stand
Hands in the sink
Hot water
Charging my vision
Senses a-prowl
And commence
My morning's meditations.

Steam
Curtains the windows,
Trees
Fringe the lawn,
Logs stacked neatly
Against a hedge.

On grass
Adorned
With relics of bread,
A birdbath,
Ludicrously warmed,
Shimmers before me.

And
Nearer still,
The stump,
Ivy'd
With ogrc-ish,
Sad,
Disney charm.
Not dead,
Nor even dying,
But once,
For a while,
Thrusting towards full
growth,

And now
Cut back.
Never again,
Unless disaster
And a glorious resurrection comes,
To approach full height again,
But cut
And cut
To fit a kitchen view.

Seasons of leaf and flower and fruit
Treasured
And loved
And lopped.

A small blue tit,
Fresh-yellow from the egg,
Hops to a branch,
Tips a bright eye,
Practices quick perfections in its pose,
Flitters,
Provokes
And flirts,
And then,
Minutely,
Shits.
Watches and waits,
Then,
Whilst my trance persists,
Is gone.

Morning moves on.
The water spasms.
My thinking wrists are cold.
Again I hear the axe,
Hear evening call,
And think how soon the day grows old.

More About Thea

Yeah, Yeah, Yeah

(Much Ado About Something)

Not much doubt about it,
Shakespeare lost a lover,
As did others too.
None of us escapes,
Yet, we all make much ado.

It really doesn't help though,
To hear our fate is shared.
Nothing that we know,
Means that we're prepared.
Death and loss still find us
With our nerve ends bared.

Another Walk

Most of the stones on this part of the walk
Are familiar, awkward, knobbly,
Preventing any pretence of smoothness in the path,
Yet smoothed themselves.
Are they truly small?
Soon to be dislodged by a casual kick?
Or mere peaks of huger, hidden masses,
Firmly set
To send the kicker sprawling?
Soon they are gone.
Gone from view that is,
As other views come in.
A line of poplars,
Eyelashes,
Awaiting the wind's meticulous brush.
Beyond them, mounds of trees,
Moulded by distance into a wood.
Old walls catch the eye,
A roofless barn,
A crop-filled field,
All busy with decline or growth,
Yet shows of permanence
Beside the fleeting traveller,
Within whom buildings burn,
Crops decay,
Wounds fester.

Thought darkens the mindscape.
Between one puddle and the next
A life keeps ending.
The air is filled with a soundless howl,
As a small catch is lifted to release a gate,
A key is turned,
A kettle filled,
A light is lit,
Another life limps on.

Home Thoughts At Home

For so many years,
Each holiday,
With or without the help of time-share sirens,
Offered its temptation
To stay, to settle,
Establish an outpost,
Even a base,
Go native.

We were easily seduced,
By views of sea and shore and sky,
The perfect house, perfectly located,
The pampering of locals,
A hotel's luxury,
Or jazz's sweet, sour squalor,
Ancient sites, with stories seeping out,
Paddleboats, on the sweep and sweat of the Mississippi,
Access to Gozo,
Cretan windmills,
Etna's smouldering rocks and buried houses,
The sleazy charm of San Francisco,
The friendly frenzy of New York.

But always home won out,
And wins out now.
A choice,
Many times made,
Is now confirmed.
Your place is here now,
Permanent,
As is mine.

For The Defence

I think I might be able to throw some light
Upon the 'younger woman' syndrome.

My memory of you is, mainly,
An amalgam of many ages.
I knew you from your age 20 to age 69,
Near 50 years.
The average, mean and median of which
Is close to 25.
Throw in the 20 you were already when we met,
Illumined for me by false memories,
Absorbed from photographs,
Of you as girl, teenager, nurse, WREN, first bride,
That gives us 45,
Which is, I think,
The composite image I carry,
Creased, in my mind's wallet,
Mature, but young,
Wise, but playful,
Some lines, but beautiful.
This is the you
I sometimes see, peeping out from passing strangers,
Or loitering friends,
Catching my eye,
Raising my interest,
Launching impossible dreams.
(They see nothing appealing peeping out from me).

Now, were you still alive,
I realise that this would all sound pretty thin,
But, circumstances being what they are,
Couldn't it be taken seriously,
As a theory, or excuse?

Your comfort can be that,
To be fixated thus,
(On 45year old infants),
Is to chase moonbeams,
Leaving me,
As always,
And forever,
With all my love,
Truly
And sincerely,
Yours . . . .

Getting Through Customs

One of the things I can't do now,
On holidays,
Is buy presents.
That was your job,
And joy.
Mine, just to pay and complain,
Look about, fidget,
Wish to be gone,
A truth, made game.

Now, if I look at market stalls,
Of T-shirts, watches, bracelets, scarves,
I feel you beside me,
Checking for loose threads,
Or other blemishes,
To bring the price down,
And the fact that you are not beside me
Is far too much,
And can't be argued down.

Bargaining was never one of my strong points.

Your price was always fixed
At the farthest reaches of my pocket.

Tell Me

Are you bothered?
Does it bother you
That I bother you still?
That I wonder,
'What would you want?
What would you wish me to do?'

Questions
I ask so often.

Other times I can acknowledge,
'Why put this burden on you?
Why ask the now long dead
To advise the ungrateful living?'

You can take neither hurt nor disappointment,
Joy nor pride.
Mine's to decide,
With just memories to guide.

One Snigger At A Time

I caught myself laughing,
Out loud,
At a line in a novel,
A wisecrack,
At the expense of one Stephanie Plum.

Maybe things are looking up,
Even though
Over-runneth,
Not yet,
Doth my cup.

If Only

If only we lived in some mythologic time.
If only it were that those Gods, in taking you,
Were punishing me for one of my many sins.
If only they could see how, pushed by adversity, I have changed,
How much better a husband I could now be.
If only they would relent and send you back.
If only you could look at this new me,
Study the changes, like what you see.
If only, like a mended fracture
We could revel in our new strength.
But,
What if those same mythologic, tyrant Gods,
Those randy sods,
Envying our new joy, our love, our luck,
Required a fierce, celestial fuck,
To leave you ravished by a swan,
Me, a buggered duck?

Postprandial

One of the things I've found myself doing this holiday,
Is having a sleep, in my room, on the bed, in the afternoons.
You used to do that.
It annoyed me slightly then.
Why pay money to cross the world, to lie in a bed,
Sleeping in day-time?

Now I do it.

I hope my old annoyance didn't show,
But, with such things, you never know for certain.
If it did, I hope not like a ripple, spreading
To disturb every quiet corner of your pool,
Or, as a vapour trail,
Thin, then filling the sky ,
To cloud your day.

If it did, pronounce your penalty,
Name your price,
I'll pay.

No Chariot, No Fire

Seeing a wheelchair, most pity the rider,
Some the pusher.
I envy the pusher.
Want to make them a special offer.
Not let them refuse.
Their task to become my task.
Their work, my joy,
As I feel again the push, the weight,
Master the precise tilt at kerbs,
The careful control on narrow paths,
Negotiating lampposts,
Dodging potholes, grills, deep pavement cracks,
Welcoming the extra effort, pushing or holding back, on hills,
Collapsing it skilfully for storage,
Looking anxiously for it at the aircraft's exit,
Or seeing it heave its untidy image into view at luggage reclaim.
Our field ambulance, armoured car, mobile canteen, shopping trolley,
Our victory bus,
Our chariot of faith and fire.
I miss the over-the-shoulder conversations,
The knowledge that you were there,
Sharing that walk, that holiday, that expedition,
Light-winged, fortune's feather,
Not today's invisible, brown burden.
Never once did I cry,
'Lords of the Universe! Let this task be taken from me!'
Many times have I cried, and cry,
'Lords! Let it be given back!'
How then these damaged knees would rejoice at their extra work.
How these now protesting feet would stride forth proudly in your service.
How my faltering gift, always hungry for more time, would find more time.
How I would charm you again.
How I would re-learn to sing, to clown, to entertain.
How the heavens would ring,
As ballads of welcome sprang from my re-born brain.

And, another thing.
Last week I stumbled and fell, outside Tesco's.
That never happened when I was pushing your wheelchair.

Let It Be Known

Let it be known that, meeting by chance,
Both of us felt that Destiny had been working overtime,
And hoped that he was adequately rewarded.

Let it be known that, since you have gone,
Half of me is unemployed,
But receives no benefits.

Let it be known that our early days
Were unbelievably, almost unbearably, ecstatic.
Emotional tanks were drained, re-fuelled, sucked dry, then filled with tears.

Let it be known that many times I behaved badly,
But am thankful that sometimes
Fools are allowed to thrive.

Let it be known that all our babes
Were works of art, that, thankfully,
Fate's art thieves never got to hear of.

Let it be known that your beauty survived through all your years,
And through three generations more, to date,
With recent additions you missed, but would have rejoiced to see.

Let it be known that you left the world full of good memories,
And that your friends are still your friends,
Your faults seen, but thrice forgiven.

Let it be known I loved you all those years
And, watered by your love,
Have grown.

Let it be known that my wound has not healed
As my voice strives
To carry your name towards the stars.

But, it must too be known that,
In striving to tell your story,
I have been ambitious beyond my gift,
As here,
I fear,
Is shewn.

Traces

Hallo rain!
Try to remember.
Cudgel your clouds for clues.
Think!
As you wash me.

Are you brother droplets
To those that chased us
Across that foreign lake?

Do you remember how we looked then?
I have photos to jog your memory.
I look. . . .
How can I put this to escape your laughter?
I look ... young, ... and fit, ... and strong.
Really,
I do.
And she?
Like a nymph,
By some strange chance
Within my thrall.

Ah rain!
How you chased us.
But I won.
I won.

As I rowed,
(That rare once, the oars obeyed me).
I could see you.
Sweeping your creased sheets towards us.
But we reached the shore
And ran,
Laughing,
Still before you,
And were settled inside,
Supping hot chocolate,
When you struck.

Surely you remember?
Or have heard of it?
Do you not exchange talk in your cloud-rooms?
Boast of drownings, floods, tsunami?
Laugh at the girlish names
They give your hurricanes?
Admit occasional defeat?

If you remember her,
Let me say....
.... it will only be
In soft brown English earth
That ever again you'll meet.

This Poem Contains Tenderness, Handle With Care

I cry less often now,
But still run into the occasional ambush,
Bursts of friendly fire,
The stealthy pang.
The last of these was from Otis Reading.
'Try a little tenderness,' he sang.

It was not the famed finale that set me off.
Not the scowling, stabbing, staccato of that ending,
So loud, so unexpected,
Not suggesting, not persuading,
But demanding, *'Do it! Do it! Do it!*
Try it! Try it!
Try a little! Try a little! Try a little!
Tenderness. Tenderness.
Do it now! Do it now! Do it now! D......'
No,
Not that bit,
But before it.
The slow, seriously sad sentiment of the beginning.
The main tune.
'She may be weary ...... try a little tenderness.'
And I reflect,
'I could do tenderness.
You did get weary
Whatever the dress,
And I got good at tenderness,'
And wonder, 'Where has it gone?
What must I do to earn ....?'

On cue, the tears come down,
Then stop,
And then, encore,
Return.

Maybe that's what happens to tenderness.
Condensed to tears,
Wasting,
Wasted,
Except to wash,
Keep clean,
Memories of those years.

Global Warning

It is quiet in the garden,
Warm in the sun.
If I sit still,
After a while,
The birds edge closer,
One by one.
When I move they fly.
My face takes joy from the heat
As I turn to watch them,
But there are holes in the sky.

Later, without a moon,
But starlit,
The heavens crumple above me.
Trees exhale, inspire;
Moles strengthen their grip upon the lawn,
Unchallenged.
In the field
Beyond the hedge,
Small creatures stalk, and fight.
Kindly, the constellations cover me,
But there are holes in the night.

The streets in town are busy.
In its own way, home is busy too.
Traffic roars through the house,
Routines are rampant,
Days have shapes
And know their place
In the calendar's queue,
Require respect.
One knit, and then one purled,
They clothe and protect,
But there are holes, great holes in the world.

Good Evening

If anything seems likely to push me towards re-mar-
riage,
Short of falling in love again, that is,
It would be these evenings,
Loathsome postscripts to the day,
When the energy is too low for work,
When tiredness beckons
With what turn out to be false promises of sleep,
When the house is empty
And the walls scream their invitation to my forehead
To beat itself against them.

I don't remember evenings ever being like this,
You know,
Before.
Neither can I remember
Our doing anything special with them,
Not latterly at least.
But now,
Each one is a challenge,
A confrontation,
A desert to be crossed,
Vacuum filled,
A turbulent, greedy sea,
A Doldrum.

They are a chunk of these last years
I could almost wish away.
Maybe I could pay them into an account,
To be drawn upon and used in the mornings;
Or give them to a charity,
A hospice,
Become a donor,
Arrange a time-transplant,
Though there could be problems of rejection,
The recipient throwing up,
Appalled at this bleak offering.

Yet, perhaps I'll moderate my curse,
Because,
The nights are even worse.

Loved You Thea

Loved you Thea.
Passing as strangers on the stairs,
Summoned to the bed-sit phone booth,
You in your robe, me in mine,
Notions humming down the line.

Taking you to student parties,
In wealthier rooms than ours, in Hampstead,
To show you off, but hoard you
Jealously, but oh so proudly.
Loved you Thea.

Carrying Carolyn on my shoulders
To the swimming pool at Purley.
Hearing her first call me 'Daddy!'
Her decision, my submission.
Loved you Thea.

You upon the bed at Carol's,
Blood-drip fixed by Doctor Mac to broomstick.
Smiling dreamily at newborn Nick,
'Am I going to die?' you asked me.
Loved you Thea.

Holding Sarah, at the window,
So Nick and Carolyn could see her,
Balanced there upon the sill.
(Children not allowed at bedside).
Loved you Thea.

In the garden, older, tired,
Grandchild's caring arms around you,
Destiny not far behind,
Prowling there amongst the fennel.
Loved you Thea.

Should have said it
Much more often,
At lunch and dinner, before breakfast.
Should have shouted (even if not from the roof-tops),
'Love you Thea!'

After loss, and pain, and grief,
After stained bereavement's face,
The silence of your emptied place,
The slow, dull ache, without relief.
Miss you, miss you, miss you Thea.

If I Were A Ship

If I were a ship,
Just setting sail,
To find you in some distant port,

How happy I'd be
To brave the wild sea
And challenge the winds at their sport.

But I know that the truth is far different,
Though sail after sail be unfurled,
No trace will there be
In all the wide sea,
Or beyond the far edge of the world.

With nowhere to search or to hide,
I must cherish the treasure inside.

Feast And Famine

When I am here, in full St Francis flow,
The patio, just outside the glass,
Is a seed street-market,
With sunflower specials,
Discounted maize,
Wheat whoppas,
Corn utopias,
Open all hours.

Back from holiday,
The dispensers long empty ,
Birds are busy still beneath them,
Pecking at grey, dishevelled earth,
Mould-mottled flagstones,
Scrambled grass.

Can there be seeds still there?
More likely just fragments, husks, detritus,
The mere scent of food,
Ghosts of nature's nurture,
Trapped in the dirt,
A memory of plenty.

Do they peck casually, to fill the time?
In joyful play?
In urgent hope?
Or ritualized despair?

Taking first cautious sniffs of morning air,
I delay my dutiful round with water, nuts and seeds,
Absorbed,
And, as they extend their search,
To peck by flowers, shrubs and trees,
So I peck, peck
At memories.

Past Imperfect

Of all the words I write,
And those I think and say,
The ones that come at night
And will not go away,

That stay to taunt and tease,
And hurt and haunt my head,
That now appear with smooth unease,
Are those I left unsaid.

Stories sweet to tell,
Shared times of love and fun,
Sadder tales as well,
Of kindnesses not done.

Who's Crying Now?

When you lived,
And tears were summoned,
It was you who obliged.
I gave support.

Now it is I
Who cries,
At every tender thought.

Story Time

Could you almost,
Nearly remember,
The way things were,
When we were younger?

The coldness of snow,
And fiery summer,
The thrust of spring
When the frosts were over?

The great white clouds
Of June and July,
Fast fat rain
From a warm, dark sky?

Autumn,
Old and grey and growling,
Bonfire blasts,
And Christmas singing?

The stealthy growth
Of winter grass,
The rescued birds
That died at our hearth?

Did you remember
How children's voices
Shredded our peace,
Made silence blessed?

Or, with a twist
Of time, or mood,
Doubled our joy,
Or tripled our dread?

All of these
You remembered well,
When we took it in turns
To listen or tell.

Now, those tales
Grow faint and bare,
Without you to listen,
To tell, and share.

Treasure Trove

The strangest thing
Is when I find you in another's memory,
Something of you I didn't know,
Recognisable
But unfamiliar,
Like left-over pieces from a re-assembled watch
I'd thought complete,
Advice you'd given,
Phrases you'd used,
Stories told,
Insights shared,
Anecdotes about me
That bring throat-thickening smiles.

No skeletons have emerged
So far.
I count my blessings.

Gardener's Question Time

Five years on,
Your face lives in photographs,
And burned in my brain.
A few more trees have gone,
A few more planted since
To take their place.

I've planted more bulbs too,
In clusters,
In the earth now opened
Where low, wide branches
Used to sweep the rain and light away.

Birds circle slowly across from further trees.
One sky-explorer
Spreads his joyous wings
To swoop and soar.
One, wise and alert for food,
Or simply tired,
Watches from the roof.
Another plunges with reckless grace towards the porch,
Hits glass,
And falls with neck awry.

Is this how the balance holds?
With one to die,
One fly,
And one to watch and know?

Flight OA 260

This time
I don't choose clouds,
But sit away from the window,
By the aisle,
Ready to escape smoothly
To the toilet
As the need becomes urgent.

Only it doesn't.
The tablets worked.

The plane half-empty,
Comfort beckons from unfilled seats.
Twitches can be indulged,
Elbows loosened,
Legs stretched out,
A coat discarded,
Then a jumper,
Both draped carelessly beside me,
My bag in the locker above,
Unburied,
Accessible.

Is this a sign?
Do happy holidays have good beginnings?

Three and a half hours to Athens.
Another tick on my list.
Trolleys come with packaged meals,
And the plastic cutlery and cups
You would always swiftly wipe
Then transfer to your handbag.
'They might be useful later.'

I enjoy the food.
We always did,
Though it is fashionable to deride it.
Those meals...
They always seemed ingenious to us,
A bonus,
Had still a sense of being treats.

I suppose the best ingredient for any meal
Is hunger.
A thought that lingers
As the hostess passes,
With a brisk swish of slim, black-stockinged legs.

How It Goes (A song- in search of a tune)

You wake one day,
When all is dark.
Somewhere there's chirping,
It's the clock.
And so it goes.
And so it goes.

Your eyes are closed,
Your fists are curled.
Somewhere outside,
The big, wide world.
And so it goes.
And so it goes.

You rise and wash,
And dress and eat.
Then push yourself
Into the street.
And so it goes.
And so it goes.

You get a job,
And earn your pay,
And learn to work,
Forget to play.
And so it goes.
And so it goes.

Or play too hard,
And get the sack,
And there you are,
Flat on your back.
And so it goes.
And so it goes.

You find a girl,
And take her home,
Then wake next morn,
To find her gone.
And so she goes.
And so she goes.

You dream a poem,
And write it down,
But, come the dawn,
The magic's gone.
And so it goes.
And so it goes.

But then one day,
You give a shake.
Years have passed,
You're wide-awake.
There's warmth and laughter
In the house,
And stroppy kids,
And watchful spouse.
Your life is full,
It overflows,
And day by day
It grows and grows.
And so it grows.
And so it grows.

You settle back,
Laze in the sun,
And thank the fates,
For all this fun.
And so it flows.
And so it flows.

But comes a day,
The fates return.
Death pays a call.
The future burns.
And so it goes.
And so it goes.

You wake again,
When all is dark.
Somewhere there's chirping.
It's the clock.
Your eyes are closed.
Your fists are curled.
Somewhere outside,
The big, wide world.
You found your girl,
And made a home.
But now you wake,
And know she's gone.
And so it goes.
And so it goes.
And so it goes.
And so it goes.
And so it goes.
And so it goes.
And so it goes.
And so it goes.

Every Day As Christmas

Some memories are strange.
For example,
With Christmas now scratching at my heart,
(And pocket),
I remember that, when I was a child,
The early-morning weight of the stocking at the bottom of the bed
Always came from an apple and, sometimes, an orange, down at the toe.

Were we so poor then that these were treats?
True, in the war, oranges were scarce, restricted, valued,
But apples!?
Were they ever in short supply?
Did we children pounce eagerly upon them?
Eat them with desperate relish?
Regardless of all the good we were told they did us?

Later, on the tree, there might be sweets,
Toys, hankies, ties or gloves,
 But. . . as to the apples,
Had they not been there
In the salvaged stocking,
We'd have missed them,
Just as so many plain, ordinary, taken-for-granted things
Are missing now.

Other Recent Poems

What's Special About Boats?

'Drowning machines,'
An old neighbour used to call them.
She regarded seasides and ports,
Margate, Southend, Yarmouth,
Grimsby, Dover,
As 'No-go zones,'
Almost foreign.

'Mark my words,' she'd say,
'If boats hadn't been invented,
 There'd be a lot less drownings.'

Her dad had been lost at sea in the war.

Mind you,
When the chips were down,
She liked her fish.

Another Valentine

Will you be my Valentine?
First move yours?
Or first move mine?

Will you be my Valentine?
Coffee at yours?
Or whisky at mine?

Will you be my Valentine?
First touch yours?
Or first touch mine?

Will you be my Valentine?
First kiss yours?
Or first kiss mine?

The world is full of people,
Many of them single.
Will you be my Valentine?

Most of them in China.
That could be a problem.
Will you be my Valentine?

You bring chicken,
I'll bring wine.
Will you be my Valentine?

Let's move together,
Keep in time,
Dream together,
Fates combine,
Try to find
The sweet sublime,
Sing soft songs
That scan and rhyme,
Exchange caresses
All the time,
Our thoughts enmesh,
Our limbs entwine,
Quick! Decide!
And give a sign.
Will you be my Valentine?

Reasons For Keeping A Diary

(as revealed to the Pub Poets, at the Crown, Downham Market)

It bothered me,
It still does,
That the years were slipping away.
Not the usual angst about getting older,
Though that too of course,
But that one's youth (and middle-age), were not just gone
But, large chunks of it, forgotten.
I could not say what happened in 1957, or '75,
Or, given an event,
Could not say which year contained it.
Could not always place a holiday,
Say which came first, which second.
Mislaid the years and months of births,
Of funerals, of parties,
Which friends or relatives we'd seen which Xmas,
Which ones we'd missed, or quarrelled with,
As though a life, full of events, was sinking without trace.
So, to stop this rot,
This composting down of separate days and deeds and thoughts,
To one warm sludge,
With just a few sharp memories,
Like eggshells, showing through,
I started a diary.

Now, if I can read my writing,
And anyone is interested to ask,
I can discover that, on Feb the something or other, 1994,
I ate breakfast, fed the birds,
Drove up to London, made visits, wrote reports,
Drove home, ate, talked, watched TV and went to bed.
Next day, dug in the garden, phoned my brother, paid some bills.
That Xmas, lots of people came.
I list their names.
At the January sales I bought some shoes, went home,
And wrote some verse,
Wallowed for 2 hours in the bath reading a novel,
Watched football on TV;
It's all here, penned down, available.

Not much about feelings do I hear you say?
I suppose that's true, and wonder why.
Perhaps because most feelings are private, concealed, withheld,
Even from ourselves,
And difficult,
Hard to set down and,
With the passing of the years,
Adopt strange forms,
Become biodegradable,
Turn soft with sentiment,
Degenerate to cliches,
Exude embarrassment,
Corrupt clean data.

No, if it's feelings you're after,
Secrets of sorrow, of joy and of pain,
Personal,
Dark,
The true inside story,
I'll give you a hint
Where you can learn more.
They no longer lie just at heart or at brain,
Slug-like and curled,
But,
In that less private core,
In poems,
In print.
Or come to the Crown,
Where all that was hid
Is revealed to the world.

The Play-off Zone

Up to half-time, we were very busy.
Kept pressing forward, retained possession.
Made intricate passing movements
It was a joy to see.
Work rate was good.
We spread the ball about, and found our men.
Were solid in defence, quick to break out.
Controlled the middle of the field.
Dictated play. Made surging runs.
We ran them ragged,
And several times came close to scoring.

The second half. . . .
A totally different game.
We lost our shape.
Made few completed passes.
Made reckless tackles.
Gave penalties. Got carded.
Made useless protests. Mike almost got sent off.
Our heads were down.
We did not perform.
Just hung on for the final whistle.

'It's been like that all season,' said our manager,
Interviewed later.
'Up.......then down.
But... ... ...I'm still hopeful.
They've got the talent.
I've just got to motivate them.
After all, that's my job... .innit?
They're a good bunch of lads.'

Our ex-manager,
Safely tucked up in his new job,
Higher up the league,
He told it different.
'They try hard enough,
They give it all they've got.
But, the bottom line? ....Well... .
They're just not good enough.
To tell it like it is....

A talentless bunch of tossers.
They should be buying-in.
But, they haven't got the cash.
Never did have the cash.
And they had the cheek to keep on blaming me!
They let me go!

But now I'm laughing.'

The commentators offered their wise words,
Cracked some jokes,
Enjoyed some laughs,
Shivered, tightened their scarves.
It was, they solemnly confirmed,
'A game of two halves.'

I think it is a life of two halves too,
With days, and hours, and minutes halved,
Not regular, but random,
The tempo always changing.

It seems possible to play two games at once,
Be up. . . and down,
On top. . . and buried,
Busy. . . but beaten,
Keen. . . but cut to ribbons,
Quick. . . but dead.
Just like the pundits said.

Siren Song

There's a new bird on the block.
Shall I stalk her?
Chat her up?
Get to know her better?
It's difficult.
So easy for her to take flight,
Misunderstand my motives.

When and where did I first see her?
I didn't.
But I know she's there.
Every morning,
As dawn creeps,
And daylight washes in to dilute my night-time fantasies,
I hear this, 'Peep... ... ...peep, peep.'
It comes from across the fields,
A dawn chorus that goes on all day,
A note of lonely desperation,
'Find me!
Find me!
I need help with my nest.
All the best locations are gone.
The price of worms is something terrible,
And, pecking and fetching
Is laying waste my powers.
My beak is sore,
My wings are killing me,
And the young ones ... ... they need a father.'

'Don't get me wrong.
There's lots of local interest,
Or I wouldn't have this lot, would I?
But. . . .peep, peep.
I want to settle down . . . . peep, peep,
Become a respectable bird-citizen,
Have holidays,
Fly south in winter,
Soak up some sun . . . . peep, peep.
It's not much to ask.
I've paid my dues,
Felt snow on my feet,

Frost on my beak,
Wind up my tail. . . peep, p...EEP,
Been flattened by rain,
Froze and felt fear as the falcon swooped,
Seen friends turned to feathered blobs on the road.
Peep, peep ... ...peep, peep.'

All day the cries go on
From the same distant spot,
Where, in the end,
My curious, impatient walk reveals to me
A constant stream of lorries
And a yellow JCB,
'Peep . . . . peep,'
Reversing on a building plot.

Hose Power

As I fiddle with this attachment,
To get the hose-pipe connected to the tap,
I know,
Because I've seen a good sample of them,
That, around the world, there are many others,
Near neighbours and further distant hose-cousins,
Doing the same.
So many, we could form a club,
Hold conferences,
Press for a seat at the United Nations.
There might be enough of us to stop a war,
Bring back happiness.

Some, of course, are connecting their hoses for criminal purposes,
Like washing their cars.
But others have business more benign, legitimate;
To water their horses, re-fill their camels,
Freshen their gardens,
Or replenish their children's pool,
Creating a rainbow spray for them to do their shrieking dance in;
Fumbling with metal and plastic to create this conduit
For the stuff of life to flow in,
Other than as nature intended.

Magicians all.

How Do You Know?

The thing is,
I don't know whether I have some sort of gift
For a distinctive style of verse,
My own,
Which is....
Well...
OK,
But which could improve as,
Well...
As I improve,
Or hope to,
And a public gets its ear tuned in,
Or whether I'm just lazy,
Can't be bothered
To put in that extra effort,
To knock it into better shape,
More recognisable,
More buyable,
More readable,
More acceptable to would-be mentors.

Perhaps I'm not lazy though,
Just self-opinionated,
Stubborn,
Questions of good or bad
Remaining open.

Teach Yourself Creative Writing

If I could just hold on to this beast,
Hold him steady,
Keep him on course,
Make him perform, produce at will,
My will.
If, always, his head and legs
Would move proudly,
His movements clean,
How much further I might travel
Towards places
Where the Gods have been.

Poems That Go Bump In The Night

Last night I slept and woke,
Tried to sleep, but stayed awake,
Then slept and woke again.

Sometimes it's a barking dog that drags in such a night,
A lorry's labouring whine,
Or party noise,
Or the clamour of an un-full, but ageing bladder
Reinforced by prostate provocation.

But often, as last night,
It is incontinence of a different order,
The swish and swirl and whirl of words
That has me reaching for pen and paper, glasses and light switch,
As multiple messages push and plop through my mental mail-box
Into a tired, protesting but greedy comprehension.

Junk mail much of it,
But often,
Bringing the same joy as the occasional cheque
Or yet more occasional fan mail,
Comes a rough idea, a trickle of ideas, sometimes a surge.

Uncertain of its worth,
I force myself to treat it seriously,
Try, through the fuddle of sleep, to write legibly,
See where it is going,
Give it a name,
Identify, if possible, a beginning, middle, and an end,
So that,
When I see it in the morning,
I find,
Not an unreadable enigma,
But, a maybe marvellous,
Maybe not-so-marvellous,
Half-familiar,
Half-forgotten,
Friend.

Up And Away

Up here,
Above the clouds,
All is whispers.
The roar of engines,
Conversation clamour ,
Trolley tattle,
All become background
To the whispering sky,
Minisculed
Between blue distance
And white, cauliflower-cloud carpet.

Journeying to new futures,
It is the past that intrudes.
Voices come from the clouds.
Trapped word visions
Tell and re-tell
Old stories,
With sound effects;
Child chatter,
Flip-flap of angels' wings,
Lost excitements,
Fantasy fodder,
Bread of heaven.

Listen!

One or other of my senses,
Or extra senses,
Keeps, lately,
Somewhat pretentiously,
Suggesting to me that,
Behind everything,
There is silence.
Not threatening, hostile, cold,
Not empty,
But a comfortable quiet,
As music fades,
Or voices taper down,
Under the murmur of domestic motors,
The body's beat,
Shifts of weather,
The hiss of winter
And the hum of summer's heat;
A waiting welcome,
A kind of shallow sleep,
Tired tranquillity,
A fellowship of peace.

Domestic Fire

It is late,
I stand on the lawn,
Staring back at the house,
At the dark back of the house,
Whose empty eyes stare starkly back at me.

Framing this confrontation,
All is ablaze,
As the plummeting sun
Hunts the horizon,
Squirting fire,
So that the sky -
Above and around the roof and walls and windows,
Still dark and glowering,
Like a sullen king
Beneath his golden crown -
Is incandescent.

The fire-red evening light
Leaps at my throat,
A Blitz bonfire,
Scorching my skin.

Whilst the heavens burn,
The house waits,
Quiet and dark,
In its own dark shadow.

Aphrodite At Ephesus

Cooked by the heat,
Our tortured feet take us,
Step by painful step,
As we learn of those who took this path
Two or three thousand years ago.
While Aphrodite shyly, boldly waits
To confront us with her body.

It felt as though we'd walked through every one of all those years
When, cool now and rested, in the Museum,
Amidst stone shapes of helmets, muscled arms,
Grave heads and stone-frozen battles,
Aphrodite, boldly, shyly,
Presented us with her body.

Temples and monuments we see;
Tributes to monsters, tyrants, cruel Gods.
Great deeds are recorded here;
Tales of calendars and kingdoms.
Their light still shines,
But paled,
Diminished by the bold, shy form of Aphrodite.

Headless, limbless,
Scratched by time,
Every aspect teases,
Tells, invites and teaches.

Then, at a small, cool shrine,
A local girl,
With just the same shy, bold beauty,
Truly, Aphrodite's daughter,
Offers to soothe us
With Magnum ice creams, Fantas and bottled water.

I Know What I Like

One wearies,
Then despairs,
Of the grosser vandalisms,
Those carried out by 'good' people,
That is - the victors,
Countries, religions, parties,
Flaunting their strength
Against temples, churches,
Paintings, statues, books,
Paying unwitting homage,
Offering their anger
To these rival gods.
Still,
That Archaic Smile,
That serene, all-knowing smirk,
I can understand the Persians
Wanting to wipe that away.

Now,
The Caryatids,
First seen by me as they holidayed,
Propping up a rather large porch
In the Euston Road,
They are another matter
Entirely.
Steadfast, far-focussed, stern,
Possibly-honest matrons,
Or maybe-maidens,
Transforming their tedious task
Into a solemn, admirable duty . . .
That's more like it.
They'll do,
In lieu,
As I wait,
Tomorrow's date,
With Aphrodite.

Seven Ages Of Grace

(A Ballad)

It was in the month of June,
The time that first we met.
Many a June has followed,
But none was better yet.

It was a kindly fate,
Decreed that we should meet.
All hail to the silver dewdrops
That danced about your feet.

By day you sweetly walked.
By night you graced my bed.
All hail to the golden glory,
That shone about your head.

You found your perfect peace,
Singing infants to their rest.
All hail to my children's mother,
With our babies at her breast.

Our children now are grown,
With babies dark and fair.
All hail to their proud grandmother,
With her tidy, silver hair.

For still her breath is sweet,
And still her step is light.
All hail to our strong matriarch
Who puts all cares to flight.

But now her eyes grow dim,
And now her movements slow,
And now she sits by the window,
Her cheeks a crimson glow,

And now my heart is breaking,
To see my lady so.

Listening Between The Lines

'I can't talk now,'
Means, 'He/She is around, both ears flapping.'

'I'm jogging along,'
Means, 'Life is hell, as usual.'

'Mustn't grumble,'
Means, 'I'm grumbling, why don't you ask me why?'

'I can't complain,'
Means, 'Why don't you listen? I've just told you. I'm complaining!'

'I expect things will sort themselves out,'
Means, 'Help! I'm drowning.'

'He/She is very good to me,'
Means .... just the opposite.

'I've a lot to be thankful for,'
Means, 'I've been cheated.'

'I must go, there's someone at the door,'
Means, 'There's no-one at the door, and if there was, I'd rather let in
an axe-murderer than go on talking to you.'

'I've had a good innings,'
Means, 'Kill the umpire, the prejudiced bastard, then hunt down his family,
and kill them too.'

The Astrologer's Apprentice

I have been watching Mars,
My first identified planet,
As he strides the sky,
Passing close,
Thrusting his frowning, warrior's face
Towards us.

For me,
Suddenly new to him,
It is as though
Only now
Have I properly joined the human race,
The brotherhood and sisterhood of Mars gazers,
Myth builders,
World shakers,
Life takers,
Destiny fakers.

Dream-work

We speak in dreams,
And dreams make speech through us.
Our lives leave clues;
Sometimes the trail is false.
A journey plotted,
But then blown off course.
A pattern, once revealed,
The fates refuse
To sanction it without a fuss.
What is becomes what seems,
And our imaginings
Create the universe.

Anniversary

A special, first-time visit,
War graves, green and white,
To find her soldier brother,
Eighteen years still, in her sight.

'I won't cry,' she said,
Approaching with small, peering steps.
'I'll be all right,'
Following the picture in her head.

But her tears heard not what she said,
As his name, patterned in stone, appeared,
And fifty years of grief,
Through ruptured eyes were shed.

Auschwitz

Between Warsaw and Krakow
The coach stopped.
It was part of the tour.
We had just passed rows of huts.

We learned they burned some of them,
At the last,
The huts.
Set fire to warehoused stores of salvaged hair,
Suitcases (each family allowed just one),
Shoes, combs,
Their careful files.

There was a heap of booties, dummies, shawls,
Taken and saved
From unsaved babies.

They broke up the ovens,
Scattered the burned and the living,
Tried to bury the unburned dead
Under the rubble,
To hide the past
And all those stolen futures.

Was it, as the tanks advanced,
Just fear?
Or had shame discovered them
At the last?

What do we bring to this place?
Our lived-in lives,
Imperfect, but intact,
Imagination,
Tears.

What do we take away?
Remembrance,
Witness,
Rage.

Who Loves You Baby?

How, in films or a play,
Are characters, often American,
Able to say, 'I love you',
It seems a hundred times a day?

For me those words are like jewels
Kept guarded in a tower,
Brought out, dusted, paraded solemnly for an hour
A few times only in a year,
To sound sincere.

And still a quiet appraiser with his eyeglass
Scans the ardent two and wonders
'Are they false or are they true?'

But then a granddaughter, to end a call, said,
'I love you granddad.'
Lightly that phrase let fall,
But as though it mattered.

How quickly are convictions shattered,
Old dogmas and proud postures battered,
Stiff upper lip reduced to tatters,
And a faltering ego flattered.

Without a pause, a shameless fool,
Upon my lips, I find the words,
'I love you too.'